CENTRIFUGAL CASTING
as a Jewelry Process

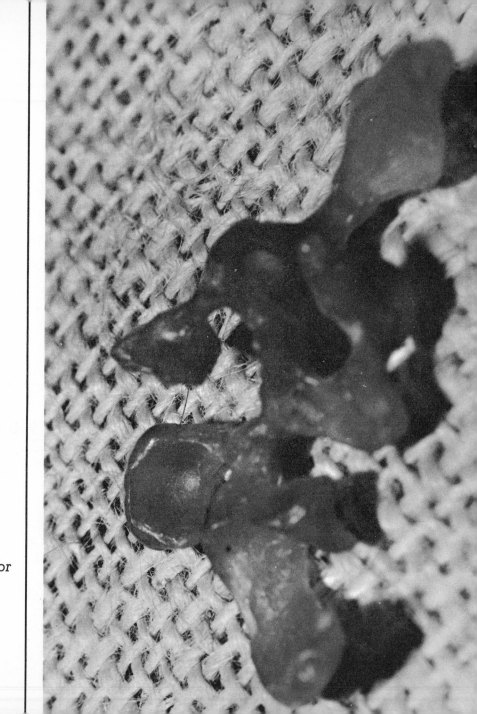

Wax model by the author

CENTRIFUGAL CASTING

as a Jewelry Process

MICKEY STORY
Instructor
Applied Arts Department
Texas Technological College

INTERNATIONAL TEXTBOOK COMPANY • SCRANTON, PENNSYLVANIA

INTERNATIONAL TEXTBOOKS IN ART EDUCATION
Italo L. de Francesco
Consulting Editor

PREFACE

The purpose of this book is to establish a comprehensive body of information that will serve as a general guide for centrifugal casting in jewelry classes in the art education departments of colleges and universities and in professional schools. Through a combination of text and photographs some of the aesthetic possibilities of the casting medium are explored. Technical information necessary for a basic understanding of casting procedures is provided. The book is written with the assumption that the reader has a general knowledge of basic jewelry terms and processes. Although it is intended as a guide for casting, this book is designed to be used in conjunction with the assistance of an art consultant.

Centrifugal casting is a medium employed by many contemporary jewelers, yet publications dealing with the subject are limited. Several current books covering the general processes of jewelry making include short sections on casting procedures, and some published information provided by manufacturers of dental casting supplies is applicable to jewelry casting. However, these sources provide only the technical information needed for casting, and no published information presently available adequately explores design as applied to centrifugally cast jewelry. This book is devoted entirely to jewelry casting as a form of artistic expression. It explores design potentialities and serves as a guide to the technical aspects of casting.

The book is divided into two sections corresponding to the two general divisions evident in the process of casting a piece of jewelry.

The first section deals with the design of a piece of cast jewelry, or the construction of a wax model. The discussion of design is drawn from 1) publications dealing with jewelry, crafts, and design, 2) experimentation by the author, and 3) statements taken from correspondence with several contemporary jewelers doing extensive work in casting. Design characteristics appropriate to the casting medium are discussed, including specific design possibilities and the techniques of working with wax. However, this design discussion is meant to serve only as a stimulus for individual experimentation and development, not as an exhaustive design survey. The text is supplemented visually with photographs of cast jewelry executed by students, contemporary jewelers, and the author.

The second section deals with the technical aspects of centrifugal casting, which includes the process of transforming a wax design into a finished metal product by forcing molten metal into a negative model mold by centrifugal force. A detailed description of the necessary steps in the technical portion of the casting process is provided in this section. Also included is an outline of the casting procedures and related information concerning supplies and the casting machine. Photographs supplement the text.

MICKEY STORY

Lubbock, Texas
April, 1963

ACKNOWLEDGMENTS

The author wishes to acknowledge the cooperation of the following jewelers who contributed information, supplied photographs, or granted permission to use photographs: Irena Brynner, Robert Engstrom, Wiltz Harrison, David Hatch, Toza and Ruth Radakovich, Christian Schmidt, and Donald B. Wright. Other individuals assisting in the study include H. J. Brennan, Lawrence Copeland, and Dr. Robert H. Wadsworth, D.D.S.

The Cranbrook Academy of Art Library was extremely cooperative in making unpublished theses available to the author.

The assistance of the following distributors of casting supplies is acknowledged: Alexander Saunders and Company, Casting Supply House, the Cleveland Dental Manufacturing Company, the I. Shor Company, Jelrus Technical Products Corporation, and Kerr Manufacturing Company.

The author is also indebted to the faculty and students of the Department of Art Education at The Pennsylvania State University for their contribution to the study and for permission to use photographs. She is especially indebted to Lester Shull for his assistance with photography.

Finally, the author wishes to acknowledge her debt to Dr. John Cataldo, advisor for the study, whose inspiration and assistance have been invaluable.

MICKEY STORY

TABLE OF CONTENTS

LIST OF ILLUSTRATIONS

DESIGN FOR CASTING

BASIC DESIGN INFORMATION

Design in the crafts

In discussing any area of the crafts, a major point of emphasis should be that of design. Because of the nature of the crafts, too much emphasis is often placed on the process. A performer in a craft can easily become preoccupied with a step-by-step progression of working procedures. Good craftsmanship is extremely important, and a knowledge of methods of working with a given material is necessary and fundamental. However, no matter how important working methods and craftsmanship may be, the importance of design cannot be minimized. Without design, process in itself would simply be manifest as solutions to problems involving construction techniques rather than as artistic expressions *through* craft media.

It is almost impossible to speak of craftsmanship, or of process in the crafts, without including design. Such a separation is a forced one and is exercised in this book *only* to emphasize a point. Actually, process in the crafts cannot be divorced from design, nor can it be separated from materials. If an expression executed in a craft medium is to be an object of aesthetic value, the design, process, and materials must be integrated to form a unified whole.

A knowledge of both material and process is important to designing in the crafts, for both will affect design and should be utilized to best advantage. The object should be designed in such a manner as to enhance and use to advantage the unique characteristics inherent in the material. With a knowledge of the working processes involved in the construction of an object in the particular material selected, the designer may also make effective and honest use of appropriate processes rather than try to force upon the material working methods foreign to its nature. The design for an object in the crafts area should be straightforward, integrating materials and processes.

A design approach enabling the designer to integrate material and process is one in which he has advance experience with the particular medium involved. The beginning designer in any craft medium should regard his first experiences as experiments to determine what characteristics the material possesses and what processes may effectively be employed. Only after the medium has been explored will the designer possess the knowledge necessary for pre-planning designs, and even then he should never hesitate to change his predetermined plan when more effective solutions to design problems suggest themselves during the working process.

And what is good design? This is a subject that has been approached from varied perspectives by many authors, with each of them expressing his own definition of good design. However, most of the authors are in agreement that a well-designed object possesses certain characteristic qualities. Related rules, or principles of design, that are comparatively common to all authors have been included in this book as a guide to assist in the formation and evaluation of designs. These five principles of design are cited briefly here as a basis for our design discussion.

1) *Function* is the first principle of design, and perhaps the most important in terms of design for the crafts. The object should be designed for its purpose. Form follows function. Since most craft objects are functional in nature, this aspect of design takes on great importance. No matter how pleasing an object may be aesthetically, if it does not effectively perform its intended function, it is not successfully designed. The purpose of the object should be considered first, whether that purpose be utility, ornamentation, or conceptual communication, and the design should proceed accordingly.

2) *Proportion* is a design principle which deals with pleasing relationships of parts within a design as they relate to the whole design. These relationships include such factors as

the relative proportions of shapes, scale, and the division of space.

3) *Balance* is the feeling of repose or equilibrium created by equal weight, tension, or interest on either side of a composition. In formal, or symmetrical, balance the weight on either side is identical and obviously equal. In asymmetrical, or informal, balance the weights on either side are distributed so as to create an illusion of repose or balance.

4) *Rhythm* is a principle of design exemplified by a sense of order and a feeling of easy movement throughout the design.

5) *Emphasis* is a fifth characteristic of good design. Emphasis lends variety and unifies the design around a center of interest or focal point.

Briefly, these five principles, when properly applied, are involved and interrelated in good design. They can be manipulated in such a manner as to create a harmonious design. However, a formula in itself is not sufficient to assure a design of aesthetic quality. A "recipe" for a design of aesthetic value must include an additional factor—that of communicative intent. Robert Von Neumann writes of this personal aspect of design:

> To instruct in design is, in a sense, presumption. Nothing is as personal as an individual's design idiom, and to write about the best way of developing a design idiom can result in gross generalities. Many authors have attempted manuals of design . . . formulas to successful design. Most have failed because they depended too heavily on the generalities and gave too little emphasis to design as a personal development.[1]

Every person has within himself a unique set of experiences which ren-

---

[1] Robert Von Neumann, *The Design and Creation of Jewelry*. Copyright, 1961, by the author. Reprinted with permission of the publisher (Philadelphia: Chilton Books, 1961), p. 185.

der him different from any other person. These different experiences work within him to form unique attitudes, beliefs, and ideas. The particular set of attributes which make up his personality become manifest in his artistic expressions. Design is not an aesthetic act when the object designed is simply the product of a detached manipulation of design elements according to prescribed patterns. Each person can put something of his character and value structure into a design, and his design can reflect his own personality.

Each individual possesses the inherent ability to create—to synthesize experiences and release untapped sources of original ideas using design as an avenue of expression. The design of a craft object should be an original act executed by means of appropriate working processes and effective craftsmanship.

Design of jewelry

In terms of jewelry design, there are few primary functional aspects to be considered, since the purpose of jewelry is essentially decorative in character. Its function is to please and enhance the personal appearance of the wearer. This general qualification leaves a wide field open for original jewelry design.

When considering limiting factors in jewelry design, the few limitations which are functional in nature deal primarily with how wearable the piece may be and with the comfort of the wearer. For example, rings and bracelets should fit comfortably and should be of a size, shape, and weight in keeping with the movement of the hands and arms. Rings, bracelets, and necklaces must, of necessity, take on a basic form because of their relation-

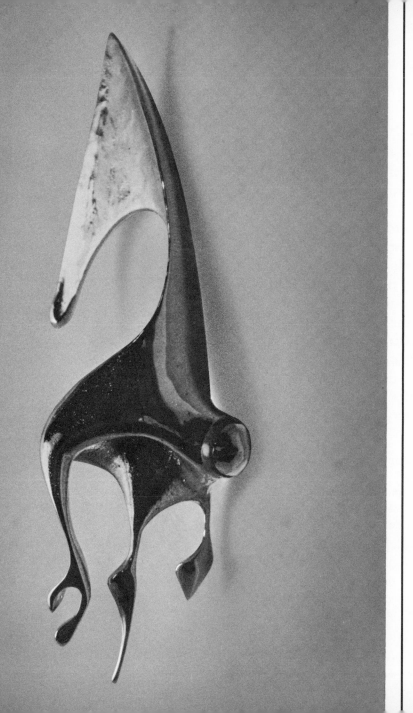

ship to anatomy, while other jewelry forms, such as pins and pendants, allow more design freedom. Generally speaking, jewelry should not be excessively heavy, so as to pull clothing or annoy the wearer, nor should it be designed with extended sharp points which could catch on clothing. Similarly, any characteristic which would cause discomfort or annoyance should be avoided. Ruth Radakovich speaks of additional functional limiting factors in jewelry design:

> There are several things that you have to think of in jewelry. One is that the piece has to stay on. Another thing is that it has to be weighted. . . . The weight has to be distributed or the piece won't sit right. . . . A pin or pendant is not looked at on eye level. On the wearer it's looked at below eye level at an angle but when you work on it you tend to work on it straight. You have to pay attention to these things.[2]

Cast pin by Ruth Radakovich in 14 karat gold with turquoise

[2] Conrad Brown (ed.), "Radakovich," *Craft Horizons,* XVIII (September/October, 1958), p. 28.

Christian Schmidt adds the following functional limitation of jewelry: "It should not be out of proportion with the human form."[3]

The majority of limitations on jewelry design, rather than being functional in nature, are imposed by the wishes of the wearer and by prevailing styles. For example, in our society jewelry is limited to cuff links and tie ornaments, earrings, necklaces, hair ornaments, and finger rings, whereas in other cultures many diversified forms of jewelry are quite fashionable.[4] Ruth Radakovich says of the jewelry in our society:

Of course jewelry can be many things. In other cultures it has a tremendous range in size, construction and function. As an art form in our culture it is one of the last to emerge from the decay of the Renaissance.[5]

Modern jewelry has, in many areas, been influenced by the more sterile forms of industrial design—such as the "stream lined" . . . designs that are so pressed into our subconsciousness that it is hard to think beyond them. But they are not part of a human 20th Century world beyond the commercial zone. The flights into space and the microscopic world are. You have the same range and choice. Things can be very personal, very delicate, or massive, majestic, huge—much jewelry (in other cultures) has been used not just to decorate, but to create a being. On festive . . . occasions a small, ordinary being becomes much more—a dramatic expression of elegance and grandeur. . . . The Jugoslav peasant dances are very slow and majestic for the women, because with all their embroidery and jewelry, they could hardly do anything else. This is an essential part of their lives. It is the human part. In many parts of the world where life is difficult and work hard—these things are the real living. Our world is neither difficult, nor is our work hard, but we suffer even more from drabness, commonness, lack of individuality.[6]

Although, in comparison with other cultures, jewelry forms are rela-

[3] Christian Schmidt, "Form in Jewelry," (mimeographed article).

[4] Von Neumann, *op. cit.*, p. 158.

[5] Ruth Radakovich, Brochure from Sculpture and Jewelry Show of Toza and Ruth Radakovich, Long Beach Museum of Art, p. 4.

[6] Ruth Radakovich, Correspondence to the author, March 21, 1962.

tively limited in our society, a wide range of possibilities still exist for individual jewelry designs. It is possible for the jeweler to simply design objects within the general framework of the types of jewelry prevalent in our culture. However, to serve as an element of individuality, jewelry may be designed especially for the person who is to wear it. Christian Schmidt states:

> Jewelry is worn on many varying situations by individuals of diverse personalities and character, and must ultimately be designed to suit or complement a particular individual.[7]

---

[7] Schmidt, op. cit., p. 2.

DESIGN AS SPECIFICALLY APPLIED TO CASTING

Development of casting as a jewelry process

Casting is rapidly becoming a popular medium among contemporary jewelers. Metal objects have been made by casting procedures for thousands of years, and it is believed that cast artifacts from early civilizations in Africa, the Far East, India, and South and Central America were the earliest examples of works done by the cire-perdue, or lost wax process. However, it has been only recently that the lost wax process was adapted to the use of centrifugal force.

Near the beginning of the twentieth century centrifugal casting was developed by the dental profession as a means of constructing crowns, bridges, and dentures. Dental casting equipment has been adapted for widely varying purposes, ranging from industrial uses to the production of jewelry. Commercial jewelers use the process for mass production of jewelry, and the popularity of the casting process with designers, craftsmen, and jewelers is growing rapidly. Casting jewelry seems to have gained momentum in the United States since 1945, when in a show of America's twenty most promising jewelers at Walker Art Center, Robert Winston's lost wax castings were the only cast jewelry shown.[8]

---

[8] Nik Krevitsky, "Winston's Cast Forms," *Craft Horizons*, XXII (January/February, 1962), p. 12.

Distinctive characteristics of cast jewelry

In considering casting as a means of making jewelry, it would be well to consider first the character of a cast piece; that is, the type of jewelry design that is appropriate to casting.

Cast jewelry should possess certain qualities which distinguish it from fabricated jewelry. If these distinguishing characteristics are not evident, no reason for casting exists. Irena Brynner says of this distinction:

> If a design is tailored or characteristic of hand-wrought jewelry, it should be worked directly in metal. There is no reason to use wax. In other words, wax should not be used to simulate hand-wrought pieces.[9]

As a method of working, casting utilizes the fluidity of metal at high temperatures, which is one of its primary

Cast ring by Irena Brynner in gold with opal (Photograph courtesy of Walker Art Center)

[9] Irena Brynner, Correspondence to the author, March 8, 1962.

qualities, and therefore, offers many possibilities for effects which cannot possibly be achieved through fabrication. These unique possibilities should be utilized rather than imitating those jewelry forms which may easily be constructed from stock silver, such as wire, tube, and flat sheet. In order to be effective, designs for casting should make honest use of the character of the casting process and the wax-working methods involved.

Casting is especially well-suited for making jewelry which has a three-dimensional quality, and is used primarily by jewelers who are involved with sculptural design values. For example, Robert Winston calls his jewelry "wearable sculptured jewelry,"[10] and Christian Schmidt's cast jewelry is said to "take advantage of the sculptural character of casting,"[11] Robert Von

Cast pendant by Toza Radakovich in 14 Karat gold

---

[10] Krevitsky, *op. cit.*, p. 12.

[11] Felt Lair, "Jewelry by Christian Schmidt," *Craft Horizons*, XX (May/June, 1960), p. 26.

Neuman says of design for casting:

> Taken as a whole, jewelry in the round rather than a flat plane concept is more effective in casting. To work in wax for jewelry one must, in a sense, adopt the sculptor's frame of reference. Since it is possible to alter mass, volume and surface at will, these elements must be invested individually and as a total, with the most sensitive and creative personality.[12]

Not only does casting make use of the third dimension, but designing an object in wax requires an entirely different concept from fabricating a piece of jewelry using rigid metal stock. As opposed to metal, wax is a soft, pliable material and is receptive to even the slightest pressures, forming easily to the design desired by the jeweler.[13] The soft plastic quality of the wax makes it especially suitable for flowing,

Cast ring by Wiltz Harrison in gold with golden citrine (Photograph courtesy of Walker Art Center)

12 Von Neumann, *op. cit.*, p. 69.
13 Von Neumann, *op. cit.*, p. 69.

natural shapes. In writing of the cast jewelry of Ronald Pearson, Daniel Rhodes states:

> Casting has given him increased freedom in the management of form. Many of his cast pieces are quite complex and bring to mind natural forms such as eroded rocks, wasps' nests, fossils, pods and plant forms.[14]

Concerning the cast jewelry of J. Arnold Frew, Conrad Brown writes:

> (Mr. Frew) feels his designs are "pretty basic," stemming from organic shapes like tree forms, natural rock formations, even the pattern that the ocean or rain makes in the sand.[15]

However, in the very character of this natural quality of wax, which may be used so effectively, lies one of the pitfalls to which so many designers fall victim. The fact that wax can

Cast pendant by Donald Wright in silver

---

[14] Daniel Rhodes, "Form in Silver by Ronald Pearson." *Craft Horizons,* XX (November/December) 1960, p. 21.

[15] Conrad Brown, "J. Arnold Frew," *Craft Horizons,* XVIII (January/February, 1958), p. 36.

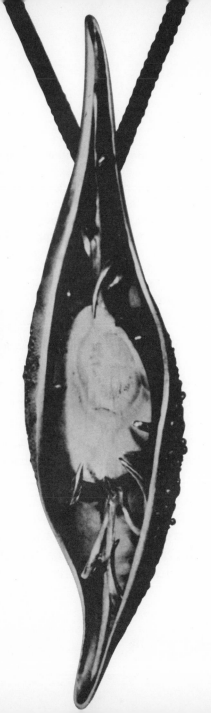

easily be formed into replicas of natural forms in existence tempts the artist to produce exact artificial copies of leaves, flowers, and countless other natural forms.

Although a form from nature may effectively be a point of departure for a design, nature should not be slavishly copied. Rather, the designer should interpret and respond to natural form and develop an individual expression of that form.[16] In the following quotation, Ruth Radakovich speaks of Christian Schmidt, who she feels has successfully interpreted nature forms in casting:

> Christian Schmidt . . . works with natural organic forms stylized to the point that they differ from nature, but they are still recognizable things. That is his interpretation . . .

Cast and fused pendant by Christian Schmidt in silver and gold with thomsonite (Photograph courtesy of Walker Art Center)

16 Von Neumann, *op. cit.*, pp. 69, 76.

of forms used as jewelry. And I think his technique is imaginative and exploring.[17]

Casting actually offers a wide range of possibilities for using individual ingenuity and imagination in terms of design. Ruth Radakovich's philosophy of design for casting also emphasizes this aspect of the process:

> There are NO ABSOLUTES. The horizon is large and the fields are fertile and barely scratched, but already people are full of rigid shoulds and shouldn'ts—A cast thing must be this or that. This is ridiculous.[18]

In his statement concerning design for casting, David P. Hatch implies the wide range of design possibilities in casting:

> My philosophy of design is that anything goes, dependent only on what it was you intended to communicate or perform. A cast piece should possess whatever characteristics assist this communication. My feeling about casting as a medium of expression are the same as for potting, weaving, etc. . . . being essentially pressed for time in the uncertain atomic age, I do things by whatever seems the most direct method with the last sacrifice of intent. So you have a ratio: "Intent" over "Method" equals "Product." In casting . . . I am trying to create the most exciting visual entity in three dimensions which is durable, with the least effort and the fewest limitations.[19]

Robert Von Neumann also emphasizes the varied possibilities of casting: "The design is limited only by the size and volume of the casting apparatus."[20] Cast jewelry may introduce variety not only through the sculptural possibilities of the wax and the plastic, natural qualities of the material, but also in the widely varied processes of working with wax. These varied processes are important to the designer working in wax because the process used influences greatly the design

---

[17] Conrad Brown (ed.), "Radakovich," *Craft Horizons,* XVIII (September/October, 1958), p. 31.

[18] Ruth Radakovich, Correspondence to the author, March 21, 1962.

[19] David P. Hatch, Correspondence to the author, March 5, 1962.

[20] Von Neumann, *op. cit.,* p. 76.

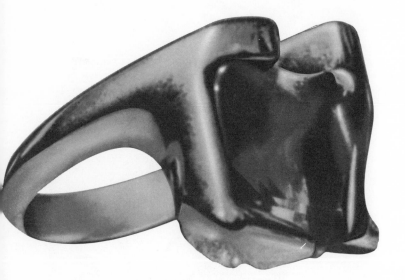

obtained. Of these varied possibilities, Irena Brynner says:

> Designing for casting, in other words, working with wax, has unlimited possibilities. I do not believe that you could say this or that style is right for casting. There are many different kinds of waxes, soft, pliable, sticky, brittle, etc. Each has its own characteristic which should always be taken advantage of.[21]
>
> I make use of the things I know I can make wax do. I heat it to a liquid, controlling its flow when I make it run, or when I drop it. I let it cool slightly and it's like toffee. I pierce it, pull it, twist it, push it, bring it up here, wind it there until I get what I want.[22]

In amplification of Miss Brynner's statement concerning the variety of methods of working with wax, a few possible procedures to be used in forming a design for a piece of jewelry in

Cast ring by David P. Hatch in gold with amber smoky topaz (Photograph courtesy of Walker Art Center)

[21] Brynner, *loc. cit.*

[22] Rose Slivka, "Irena Brynner," *Craft Horizons*, XIX (March/April, 1959), p. 33.

wax will be discussed here. The various types of wax which she mentioned will be dealt with later.

Basically, the majority of techniques to be discussed seem to fall into two categories. Either they are of a subtractive, or carving, nature or they are of a building, or additive, nature. In those techniques of working which are considered subtractive, the desired effect is achieved by beginning with a basic piece of wax and removing wax in excess of that required for the design. This removal may be accomplished in a variety of ways. It may be carved or cut away with a sharp carving instrument either by heating the tool or by simply using the tool cold. If a heated tool is desired, it may be held for a few seconds over the flame of an alcohol lamp or a Bunsen burner.

A plastic, claylike working quality may be attained in the wax by heat-

Cast pendant by Donald Wright

ing it to a temperature which will soften the wax, but not melt it. This degree of heat may be achieved either by placing the wax directly below an infrared lamp or an electric light bulb or by immersing it in warm (not hot) water for a short period of time.

Another effect achieved with heat is that of actually melting wax from the piece on which one is working. This will produce a different subtractive effect than removing wax by carving.

Very hard carving waxes may be treated in a subtractive manner by the use of processes which one would generally associate with working in a more rigid material, such as wood. Of this method of working, Ruth Radakovich states: "(The hard carving wax) has plastic resin in it. . . . You have to carve the form. It's almost like wood."[23]

Cast pin by the author

23 Conrad Brown, "Radakovich," *Craft Horizons*, XVIII (September/October, 1958), p. 26.

With drills, files, and abrasives, as well as carving instruments, it is possible to attain a very high degree of refinement in the wax stage thereby eliminating much filing and polishing in the more difficult metal stage. Hard carving wax can also be turned on a metal lathe. A metal rod about ¼ inch in diameter may be dipped repeatedly into hot wax to build up a cylinder as though one were dipping a candle. Unfortunately, wax cannot be cast into a long cylindrically-shaped mold without cavitation in the center due to shrinkage of the wax in cooling. After the wax shape formed by dipping has hardened, the bare end of the metal rod is secured in the lathe chuck and the wax is turned at low speed using a cutting tool, as a graver. A final smoothness is obtained by the use of a dull instrument, such as a spatula, to

Cast pin by Donald Wright in sterling

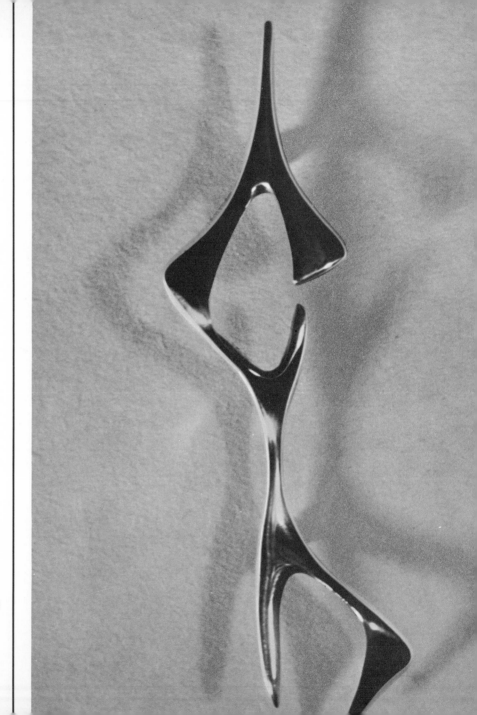

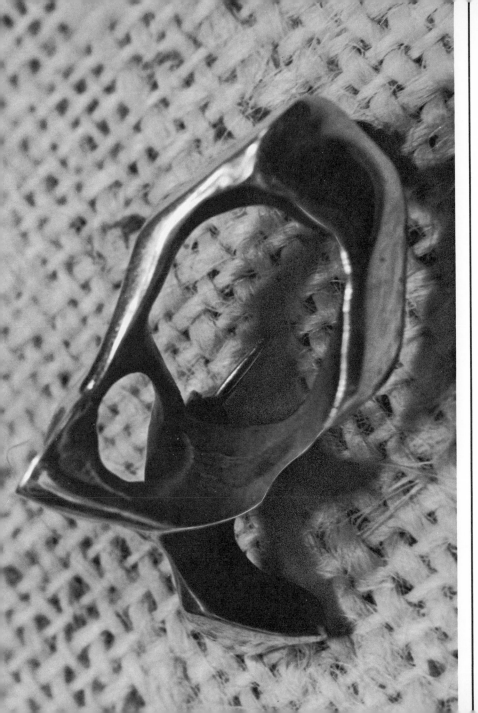

scrape rather than cut the wax. A pre-cut template of thin metal will assist in accurate production of a design in wax. The metal rod can be withdrawn from the finished wax model by slowly heating the tip of the rod with a torch and carefully pulling the rod from the wax at the moment it is hot enough to release. Because of high heat conductivity, a hard copper or silver rod is best to use; steel will not work. When the rod has been removed and the wax allowed to cool, the hole left by the rod may be filled or, perhaps, hallowed out even more to obtain a lighter finished casting.[24]

The additive processes include all those methods of working in which wax is added to the basic piece rather than carved away from it. The design is built up gradually by using heat to join separate wax shapes, or wax may

Cast pin by the author

24 Donald Wright, *Centrifugal Investment Casting for the Artist-Craftsman*, Bloomfield Hills: Cranbrook Academy of Art Library, 1958, p. 12. (Publication permission by author and Cranbrook Academy of Art).

be flowed onto the piece either from another piece of wax which has been heated or from a heated spatula used to pick up the wax and melt it. Wax wires may be very helpful in this manner of working. They may be used to build up delicate and fine linear areas of a design.

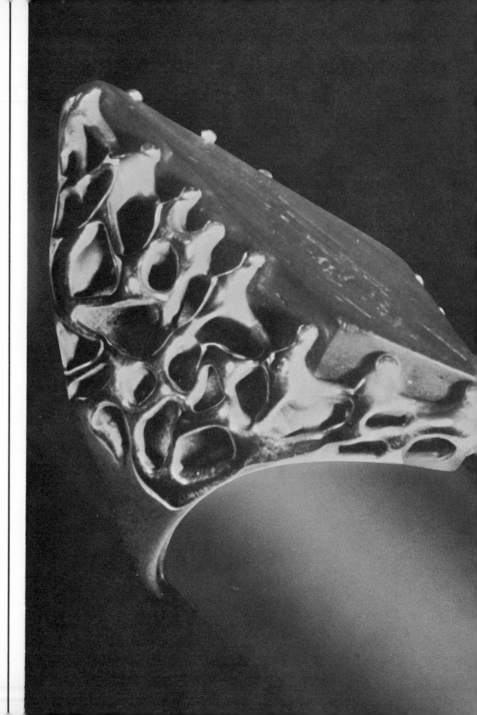

Cast ring by Donald Wright

Cast ring by the author

Textures may be incorporated into the design in a variety of ways. Soft wax may be textured by pressing objects into it. Hard wax may be incised or engraved with carving tools. Melted wax may be poured on a textured surface which has been lubricated with either a light machine oil or a professional casting lubricant, then removed from the surface after cooling and hardening. Textures may also be obtained by dripping melted wax on a model. The texturing process of granulation which is described by David Hatch as a "technical pushover" in casting may be achieved by using a bit of piano wire to apply minute wax spheres to the surface of a model.[25]

Cast pin by Irena Brynner in gold with opal (Photograph courtesy of Walker Art Center)

[25] David P. Hatch, *loc. cit.*

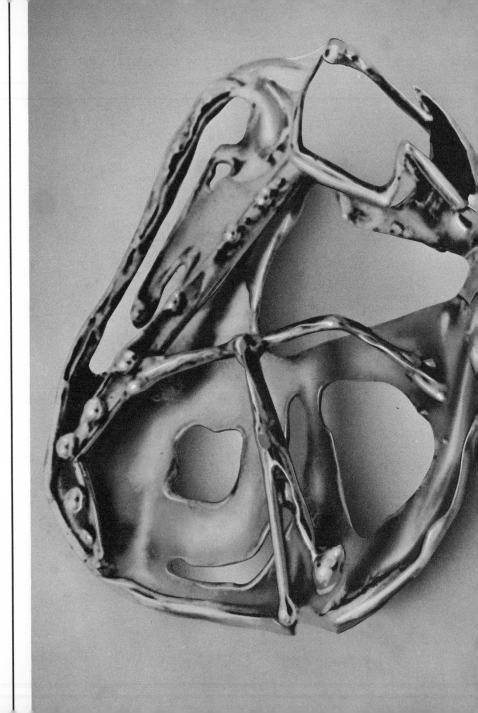

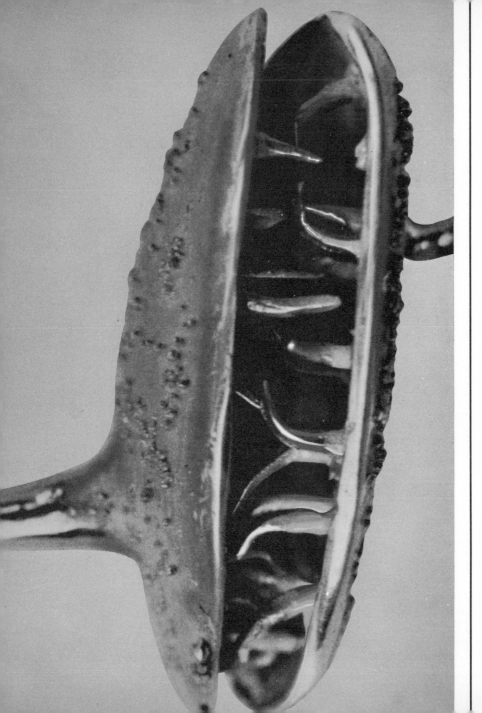

Detail of cast gold pin by Toza Radakovich

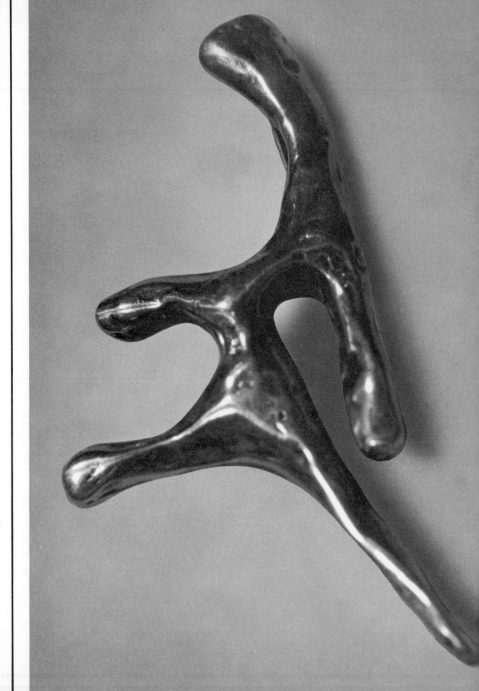

Cast sterling silver pin by Isabel Parks

Cast pendant by Christian Schmidt in silver and gold with thomsonite (Photograph courtesy of Walker Art Center)

A number of "accidental" methods may be employed in the formation of a design in wax. A variety of interesting forms may be created by pouring melted wax from various levels into a container of cold water. Forms may also come forth as a result of pouring layers of melted wax over a lubricated form.

Robert Winston has conducted design experiments using casting investment. It is possible to build up quite involved jewelry forms, Mr. Winston has found, by using an investment core as a skeletal structure to hold a wax shape which has inner, as well as outer detail. Winston occasionally shapes a piece of investment and hammers or carves a design directly into it. Wax is applied to the investment, capturing a negative impression of the

Cast pendant by Donald Wright utilizing "accidental" design method of pouring melted wax into water

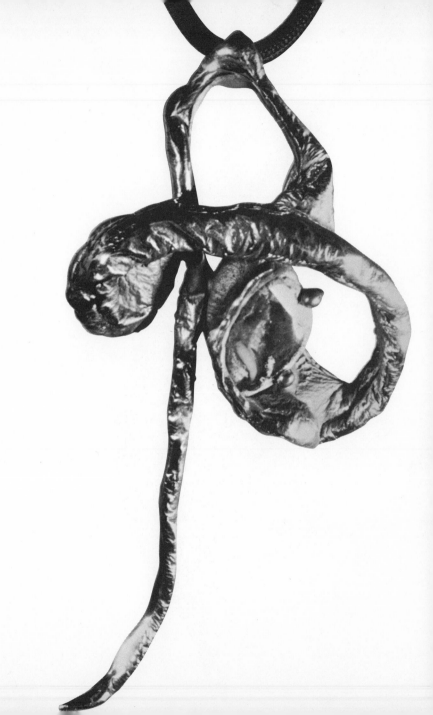

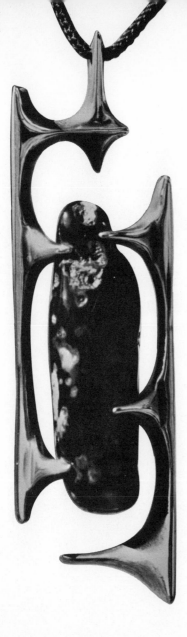

carved design. The piece is then cast in the usual manner.[26]

Robert Winston has also successfuly cast one metal to another; for example, he may make a wax model and cast it in bronze. With the bronze casting complete, wax additions are made to the detail, then the additions are cast in silver, fusing to the previously cast bronze.[27]

The familiar jeweler's dapping block may be used in casting to form hollow, half-round forms from sheet wax. The forms may be applied to a wax model as domes or combined to form spherical shapes.[28]

Stones may be incorporated into wax designs in many ways. Originally stones were coated with a lubricant before being incorporated into the desired setting in the wax model. Once

Pendant cast in sterling, with agatized coral, by Donald Wright

[26] Krevitsky, *op. cit.*, p. 11.

[27] Krevitsky, *loc. cit.*

[28] Wadsworth, *loc. cit.*

the setting was complete, the model was softened in warm water, and the stone removed by the use of a small stick secured to the top of the stone with sealing wax. After the casting was complete, the stone was replaced and the metal tightened around the stone. For many types of stones this is still the best procedure. However, some contemporary jewelers have experimented with direct casting around stones. They have discovered that some stones may be successfully treated in this way. Robert Von Neumann states that stones of a hardness of at least eight on the Mohs scale are suitable for direct casting,[29] while David P. Hatch recommends diamonds, rubies, sapphires, and synthetic stones with a hardness of seven or greater.[30]

Ring by Stan Phillips using silver with synthetic stone cast in place

[29] Von Neumann, *op. cit.*

[30] Hatch, *loc. cit.*

*Ring cast by the author in gold
with ruby set after casting*

Robert Winston also suggests synthetic stones for this process, and he adds jade to the list of natural stones appropriate to the process.[31] In casting around stones, the mold should be heated slowly and steadily in melting out the wax, and after casting, it should be cooled like glass in a kiln, using no water.

If a design for a ring is planned, it may be helpful to form the wax model on a ring mandrel or dowel which has been sized by building it up with masking tape. A layer of tracing paper, wax paper, microfilm, or tin foil under the ring will facilitate its removel from the mandrel or dowel at the completion of the design.

In regard to the size of the ring model, it may be wise for the designer

[31] Krevitsky, *op. cit.*, p. 12.

to make the model slightly smaller ($\frac{1}{4}$ size if shank is smooth) than the desired size of the finished ring, for although the ring seems to shrink a little in the casting process, considerable metal may be removed from the inside of the ring during the refining process. For the same reason, it may be desirable to leave the shank of the ring slightly thicker than desired in the final product. It is easier to make a ring larger than smaller.

If the wax becomes too soft for effective working during the forming of the model, one may find it helpful to submerge the piece in a shallow bowl of cold water. In a very short period of time the cold water will cause the wax to return to a firm state for working.

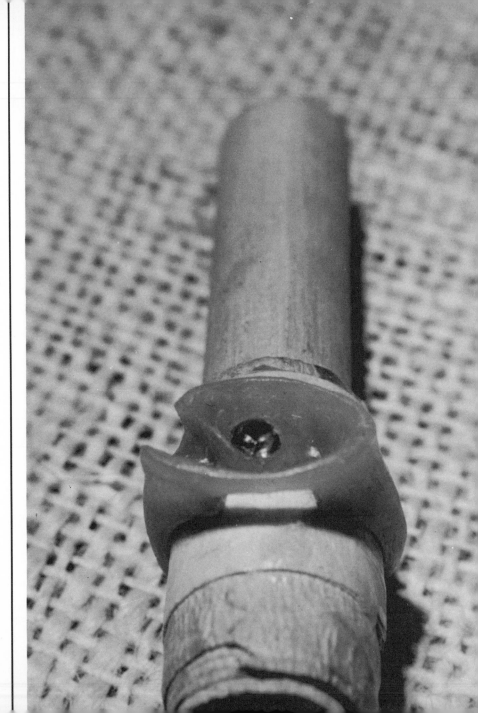

Ring model in wax formed on a dowel

In considering design possibilities, the feasibility of combining cast forms with constructed parts to make up a single piece of jewelry should not be neglected. Processes of fabrication, fusing, and forging may be integrated quite effectively with casting to form a unified design.

Pin by Toza Radakovich combining casting, forging, and construction processes

Detail of cast pin by Toza Radakovich combining construction processes with casting

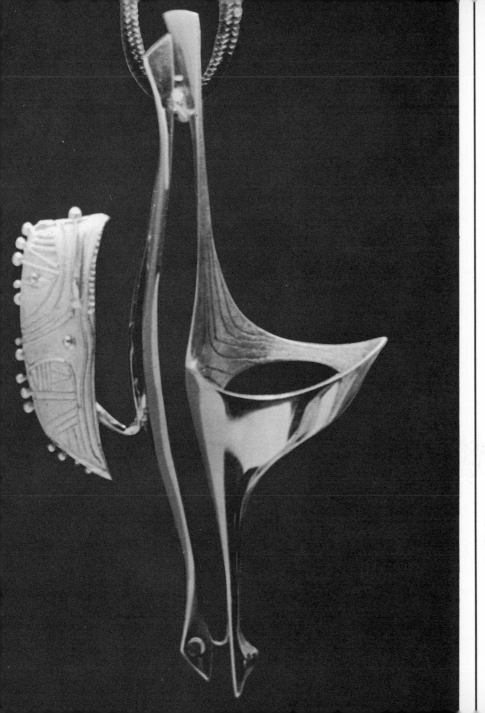

Pendant in gold by Toza Radakovich combining the forging process with casting

Two approaches to design

Through the use of various wax-working processes the first step in the centrifugal casting process will be accomplished, that of designing and constructing a wax model of the object to be cast. This may be accomplished either by a preplanned approach in which the design is first sketched, then constructed three-dimensionally in wax, or by an evolving approach in which one simply begins working with the wax, allowing the design to evolve as he works. In either case, during the working process one should be aware of the constantly changing characteristics of the wax model as well as his own changing ideas, and should be alert to changes which could enhance

Beginning stage of wax model in progress

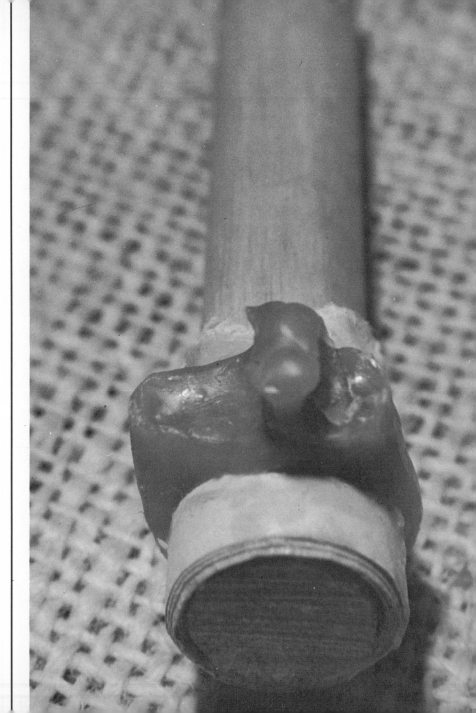

the piece. Even if a piece has been pre-planned, one should not hesitate to change the original plan as new forms and ideas emerge during the working process.[32]

John Dewey describes such changes in design resulting from working processes:

> Everyone knows that (the form) must undergo change. It is not so generally recognized that a similar transformation takes place on the side of the "inner" materials, images, observations, memories and emotions. They are also progressively reformed.[33]

Wax model in progress

[32] Gordon Lawson, *Form in Silver*. (Bloomfield Hills: Cranbrook Academy of Art Library, 1950), p. 4. (Publication permission by Cranbrook Academy of Art).

[33] John Dewey, *Art as Experience*, (New York: Minton, Balch & Company, 1934), p. 74. (Reprinted by permission of G. D. Putnam's Sons)

Experimentation

Seldom is a design in wax for a piece of jewelry completed without the use of a number of methods of working with wax. It should be noted that the author has not attempted in this book to describe all the possible techniques of waxworking. These methods of working are only basic techniques designed to serve as guide lines and to help set the person working in wax on the path of his own best thinking and experimentation with the medium. Many times an original method of working will evolve into an original design. Conrad Brown, when speaking of Henry Shawah's attitude toward experimentation in jewelry processes, says:

> A little quirk you stumble over sometimes opens up whole new vistas of design . . . or

Wax model in progress

you get a design in your head that calls for the development of a brand new technique.[34]

As the designer experiments with wax he learns to use evolving techniques to capacity and to control each technique in order to achieve the many effects he desires.

However, experienced jewelers warn that the designer should not become preoccupied with technique experimentation only. Ruth Radakovich states:

> There is one danger with the "experimenting" . . . approach . . . and that is the tendency to consider these things the goals —they become rather sacred. They are not. A piece may be new and very bad. Experimenting . . . has some concrete goal at the end of it. True experimentation is a very disciplined thing; done with a great deal of thought . . . and for a definite purpose.

Experimenting is to think beyond the present limits of the mind.[35]

Christian Schmidt says of technique experimentation:

> To be of value to an artist, a technique must be mastered to the extent that it is no longer a self-conscious effort which hinders the expression of the artist's concepts. Mastery of a technique does not guarantee sound artistic results any more than the mastery of a language guarantees profound literary efforts.[36]

Although the first experience with a wax model may be successful, and a design in wax produced which, when cast, results in an aesthetically pleasing, well-executed piece of jewelry, it should be emphasized that much experience with the process is necessary before skillful control of the medium and confidence in the medium are achieved.

---

[34] Conrad Brown, "Henry Shawah's Jewelry is a Compliment to Beauty," *Craft Horizons,* XIX (September/October, 1959), p. 33.

[35] Ruth Radakovich, Correspondence to the author, March 21, 1962.

[36] Christian Schmidt, Correspondence to the author, March 24, 1962.

SUPPLIES FOR FORMING
A WAX MODEL

As mentioned earlier, several types of prepared casting wax are available for use in the construction of wax models. These prepared casting waxes are made up of combinations of mineral and organic waxes and gums. These waxes may be carnauba, candelilla, beeswax, and spermaceti, all organic waxes, and paraffin as a mineral wax. The gums are mastic, copal, dammar, and resin. The required factor in a casting wax is that it must burn away without leaving a residue. Although many types of casting waxes are available, for all practical purposes these waxes fall into two categories or are a blend of the two—hard carving wax and soft blending wax. The hard wax has a good carving surface and is used in instances when a design of a carved or incised nature is desired.

Soft blending wax, ordinarily supplied in bulk pieces, is soft, pliable, and plastic and is used in sealing joints and in adding thickness to designs. However, soft blending wax is probably most frequently used in mixture with hard carving wax. The proportions vary according to the anticipated use to lend various degrees of softness and pliability. It is an equal mixture of the two waxes which seems most practical for the majority of design problems in centrifugal casting. Such a mixture takes on the desirable characteristics of both waxes and allows the designer to bend, shape, and mold the piece, yet he is able to carve it to achieve an incised effect. There are occasions, however, when either the hard or the soft wax may be more appropriately used alone for a particular design solu-

Commercial casting wax

tion. With experience the designer will be able to determine which wax or mixture of waxes will do each job most effectively and efficiently.

Wax is available in the following shapes: wax wires, sheet wax, and block form.

Wax wires are available in assorted gauges corresponding to the Brown and Sharpe gauge. The wires are soft, durable, and pliable and may be easily bent and twisted in the design process, as well as heated, melted together, and so forth. Although the use of the wires alone might prove to be a limiting factor in the design process, the wax wires may be extremely helpful in forming those areas in a design which are particularly delicate. For example, they may be used for forming the bezel for stones or for shaping

Hair ornament cast by the author in sterling silver

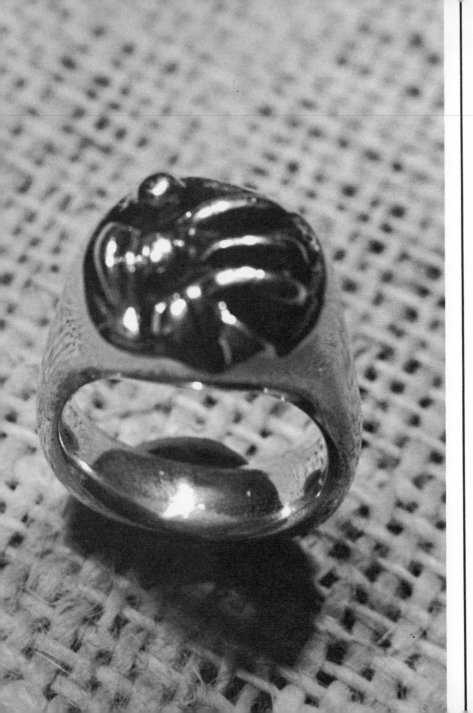

a delicate shank or a band for a ring. Because the wax wires are soft, they do not lend themselves to carving. However, if a carving surface is desired, melted hard carving wax may be added to the wires with a heated spatula. When cooled, the harder wax may be treated with carving tools.

Wax sheets are available in varying thicknesses also corresponding to the Brown and Sharpe gauge. This is usually a relatively soft blend of waxes which can be carved, as well as shaped. Wax sheets, particularly those of a heavier gauge, will generally offer more design possibilities than will wax wires. Almost all grades of wax, in terms of hardness or softness, are available in a bulk or block form. When using the block shape the designer is hardly limited at all by the original

Cast sterling silver ring by Carol Coss

wax shape, because he can simply cut from the block any desired size and thickness of wax from which to work.

Manufacturers use colors in waxes to provide codes for properties such as size, hardness, and melting point. However, these colors are reliable only within the stock of one particular company, for the color code varies from manufacturer to manufacturer.[37]

If professional waxes are not available, the designer may prepare his own wax in a quite satisfactory, yet inexpensive, manner. Some craftsmen prefer to do this. Beeswax and paraffin should be mixed in equal parts by melting the two types of wax in a double boiler. The beeswax acts as a soft wax, while the paraffin counteracts its softness, lending carving characteristics to the blend. This

Cast sterling silver ring by Rose Maust

wax forms a good general purpose wax similar to that obtained by a mixture of hard and soft waxes which is obtained commercially. After heating the wax to its melting point, it may be cooled on glass plates. These plates should be coated beforehand with a commercial casting lubricant or a light machine oil to prevent the wax from adhering. It may also prove helpful to build up a clay wall around the edge of the glass in order to control the melted wax as it is poured on the glass. After sufficient cooling, the hardened wax may be cut into squares or strips and removed from the glass slab with a spatula.

In addition to wax itself, other supplies will also be needed for forming the wax model. An alcohol lamp or a Bunsen burner is ideal for heating wax during the construction stages.

Casting wax made from bees-wax and paraffin

Candles and various flames produced by gas appliances are adequate for this purpose, but they produce soot which discolors the wax. In some cases this carbon residue may cause the final cast metal surface to be rough and porous. To avoid this, a yellow reducing flame should not be used for waxworking.[38] As mentioned earlier, if a clay-like consistency is desired in the wax, a hot plate, electric lamp, or a container of warm water will be required for heating purposes.

Various tools will be needed for carving and shaping the wax. Wax tools are produced commercially in two types: spatulas and carving instruments. The spatula has a thin handle with a small shallow spoon shape on one end or at times on both ends. The carving tool is similar in shape to

Alcohol lamp to provide heat for forming a wax model

[38] Von Neumann, ibid., p. 76.

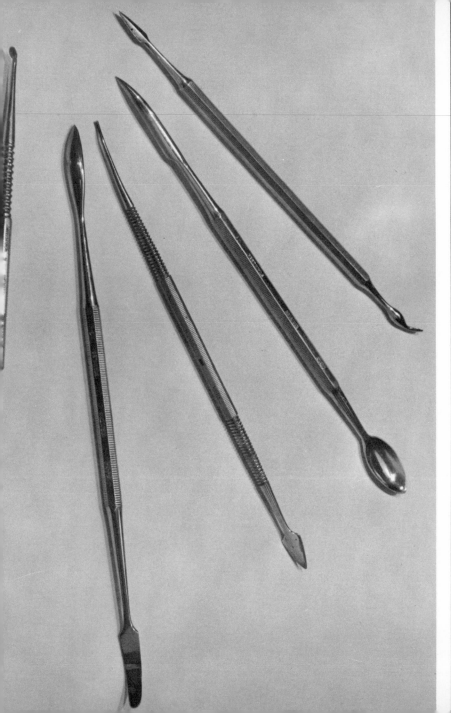

the spatula except that either end terminates in a blade—one dull, the other thin and sharp. The dull blade is used for scraping away wax, while the thin sharp blade performs cutting and incising operations.

If professional tools are not available, instruments may be improvised from other art work tools such as those used for woodcuts or linoleum blocks. Quite satisfactory tools for working with wax can also be made from nails or 14-gauge steel, copper, or brass wire by planishing and polishing the ends of 5-inch pieces of the wire to spatulate tips of desired shapes. A heavy sewing needle fixed into a section of doweling or a mechanical pencil is an ideal tool for delicate areas.[39]

Commercial tools for forming a wax model

[39] Von Neumann, *op. cit.*, p. 76.

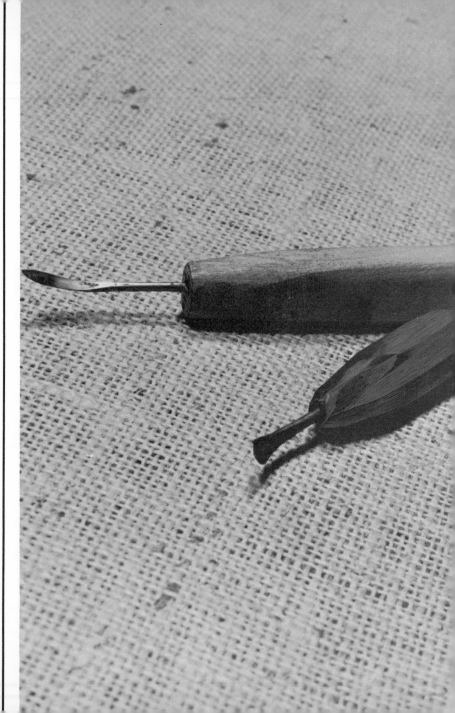

Waxworking tools improvised from nails and wire

REFINING OF THE MODEL

The design which eventually emerges as a wax model for a piece of jewelry should be as nearly as possible an exact model, *in scrupulous*

detail, of the piece of jewelry as it is expected to appear in its metal form. When successfully cast, the metal piece will come from the mold identical in every detail to the wax model, and any additional changes or refining can be accomplished only by metalworking processes. All refining except final smoothing and polishing can be more easily accomplished in the wax stage than in metal after casting. However, very delicate parts may be more easily refined in metal after casting.

When the wax model has been developed to the desired design, there are several processes by which the surface of the piece may be refined or smoothed. The piece should be carefully burnished by lightly rubbing it with a blunt, cold tool to pack the wax and to eliminate loose wax, air pockets, pits, and so forth. Even if a textured surface is desired, it is advisable to pack the wax as well as possible without distorting the texture.

The piece may be further refined in a number of ways. It may be held under cold water and brushed with cotton or a fine, soft brush. A warm wax model may be polished with a small cotton wad which has been dipped in water and passed through a flame. Cold wax may be smoothed with silk, a piece of well-used chamois leather, or fresh clean emery paper of number 1 and number 3/0 cut.[40] Another smoothing method which may prove helpful is that of rubbing the model with cotton moistened in kerosene.

Heat may also be used in this final smoothing process. A large model may be smoothed somewhat by passing it quickly over the flame of an alcohol lamp. Heat may be applied in a more controlled manner by using matches. However, a more effective method of smoothing by heat is accomplished by attaching a hypodermic needle or an eyedropper to a rubber hose through which gas flows to form a very small flame.[41] Another effective way of smoothing a wax model by controlled heat is through radiant heat. A piece of wire like that used in the heating element of an electric toaster or hot plate is attached to the handle of an old soldering pencil. The glowing tip of the wire may be held near the surface of the wax for a quite controlled smoothing effect.[42]

Some craftsmen prefer to cast a relatively rough wax model and refine the piece after it is cast, using files and abrasives.

---

[40] Von Neumann, *op. cit.*, p. 76.

[41] Von Neumann, *op. cit.*, p. 78.

[42] Wright, *op. cit.*, p. 11.

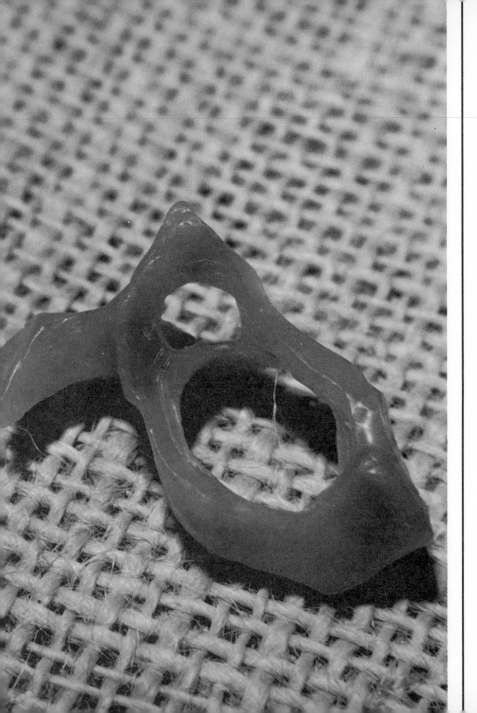

TECHNICAL ASPECTS OF CASTING

SPRUEING

When the desired degree of refinement has been achieved in the wax model, wax wires called sprues should be attached, and the model should be mounted on a sprue former (i.e., a circular metal or rubber plate with a cone shape in the center). After the wax model is encased in a mold and the wax melted out, the wax sprues will form in the mold hollow channels through which molten metal will flow to the negative space originally occupied by the wax model. Because of the importance of the function of these channels, all sprues should be carefully formed and attached.

The number and size of sprues depends upon the size and shape of the wax model, but sprues should always be as short as possible in order to limit the distance the metal must travel during the casting procedure.

Wax model, with sprues attached, mounted on metal sprue former

Eight gauge round wax wire is usually recommended for sprueing unless the model is too small to carry it. A minimum size of 14-gauge round wire should be used to prevent the solidifying or freezing of sprues before the required amount of metal enters the mold.

One end of the main, or central, sprue should be carefully sealed to the heaviest portion of the model. In the case of rings, the main sprue is usually secured to the shank opposite the top. A "button" three-eighths inch in diameter should be built up on the main sprue at a point one-fourth inch below the joining of the sprue to the model. The cone of the sprue former should be filled with wax, and the free end of the main sprue of the model should be attached to the wax in the cone former through the hole in the sprue former.

Once the model is held in position by the main sprue, supplementary auxiliary sprues may be attached to the model as needed. The number depends upon the particular model. These sprues will merely be extensions from the cast piece which, after casting, can be removed easily with a jeweler's saw, files, or cutting discs.

Sprues should be refined so that their surface is as smooth as possible. Their sides should be parallel, broadening slightly where they join the model. Points of juncture should be without sharp corners, forming in the investment continuous channels through which molten metal will flow freely during casting.

If desired, multiple castings are possible. Several models may be mounted on the same sprue former

Wax models with sprues attached to sprue former in preparation for a multiple casting

with sufficient sprues for each. Care should be taken that none of the models touch. The number of models which may be cast at one time is dependent on—1) the size of the flask,—2) the amount of molten metal which the crucible will hold and—3) the temperature level of the available equipment for heating the metal.

Determining the amount of metal

Before encasing the wax model in a mold, it is necessary to determine the amount of metal which will be needed for the casting. The person who is experienced in casting can usually estimate successfully the amount of metal needed for a model. However, the exact amount may be determined either by water displacement or by weight.

The correct amount of metal for a casting as determined by water displacement

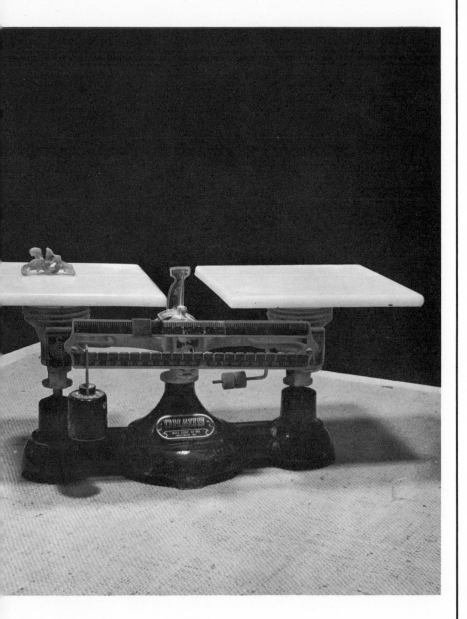

In the water-displacement method, the wax model is attached to a wire and submerged in a container of water. After the water level has been marked, the wax model is removed. Then sufficient metal is submerged in the water to bring the water up again to the marked level. Adhesion and cohesion factors add some unreliability to the water-displacement method.

In using the weight method, the amount of metal is determined by multiplying the weight of the wax model and sprues (before attaching sprue former) by the ratio of metal weight to wax weight. This ratio is determined by weighing equal amounts of metal and wax or simply by finding the ratio of the specific gravity of the metal to the specific gravity of wax. The accompanying table provides the specific gravity of many metals used

The amount of metal for a casting as determined by weight

in the casting of jewelry, and in practice, will actually provide the ratios of the metals to wax since the specific gravity of wax is approximately one.

Wax	1.0
Platinum	21.4
Nickel	8.7
Sterling silver	10.29
Nickel silver A	8.75
Brass	8.40
10 K Yellow gold	11.73
14 K Yellow gold	13.18
18 K Yellow gold	15.28
14 K White gold	13.78
18 K White gold	14.7

Using the table, the following formula may be employed:

Weight of wax model $\times$ Ratio of metal weight : wax weight = Amount of metal required for casting.

For example, if a model weighing 3 grams is to be cast in 10 K yellow gold (specific gravity 11.73), the ratio of the metal weight to wax weight is 11.73:1. Therefore, the required metal for the casting is 3 grams $\times$ 11.73 = 35.19 grams.

If a model weighing 2 grams is to be cast in sterling silver, the weight of the metal for the casting is determined as follows: $2 \times 10.29:1$ = 2 grams $\times$ 10.29 = 20.58 grams.

If desired, metal may be measured before sprues are attached to the wax model. However, if this is done, a minimum of $\frac{1}{2}$ ounce of silver or $\frac{3}{4}$ ounce of gold should be added to the measured amount to assure that the sprues and the sprue button will be filled.

Debubblizing

The wax model should be painted with a wetting agent, or a

debubblizing solution, which relieves the surface tension of the water so that the mold material will flow uniformly around the model, adhere to it firmly, and reproduce the model accurately. This debubblizing liquid will provide a smoother surface on the cast piece and eliminate nodules caused by air bubbles remaining between the wax and the mold. Commercially prepared debubblizers, a liquid detergent, or a mixture of green soap and hydrogen peroxide may be used.

The solution should be applied carefully so as to avoid formation of air bubbles. Flowing the liquid on with a soft brush is more effective than applying it with a scrubbing motion. The model may also be dipped into the debubblizing solution several times to be sure that it is well-coated.

Painting a wax model with de-bubblizing liquid

Selecting the flask

An appropriate flask should be selected for the casting depending on the size of the wax model. The flask, a metal cylinder (usually steel), will hold the investment material in which the wax model is encased to form a mold.

A variety of commercial flasks are available. Some small casting is done in flasks made of brass. However, larger, heavy duty flasks are ordinarily made of stainless steel because brass tends to oxidize under heavy use and melt at very high temperatures. Professional casting flasks are available in varying sizes and diameters ranging from dental casting flasks, which are approximately the size of a thimble, to industrial flasks twelve inches high and six to eight inches in diameter.[43] Any type of professional flasks

Professional casting flasks

[43] Von Neumann, *op. cit.*, p. 78.

which is appropriate to the particular casting may be used in jewelry casting, provided it fits the centrifuge.

The selection of a flask should be made on the basis of the size of the wax model and the size of the centrifuge. When the flask is centered over the model mounted on a sprue former, the model should clear the walls by one-fourth inch for a very small flask to one-half inch for a larger flask. The top of the model should be below the level of the top of the flask by a minimum of one-fourth inch to one inch or more depending on the flask size. This clearance will allow room for mold strength and thickness sufficient to withstand casting pressure. Although the flask must be large enough to allow the proper amount of clearance on all sides, it is not wise to select a flask which would allow a great deal more

Wax model inside flask, showing proper clearance

space, for the larger the flask and the greater the amount of investment, the longer the period required for the wax to completely burn out of the mold. Ideally, *the smallest flask possible should be used*, and the flask should have the thinnest wall possible with adequate strength to withstand the process.

If it is found in selecting a flask that the model is too large to fit inside the largest available cylinder, the model may be cut with a sharp, warm, thin blade, and the pieces cast in separate flasks. The pieces can then be rejoined by soldering after they are cast.

If stainless steel flasks are not available, an ordinary tin can with both ends removed may be used for a flask. Tin-can flasks may be desirable when the wax model is of a size which does not readily fit into a cylindrical flask. The tin flask may be bent to accommodate unusual shapes not possible in a rigid steel flask. If necessary, a large tin can may even be cut down to accommodate a model. Sharp burrs should be filed down, and the flask bound with heavy iron wire.[44]

The flask selected should be lined with strip asbestos. A one-fourth to one-half inch shortage in the width of the asbestos strip will leave the flask edges exposed so that the mold material will be locked into the flask when subjected to the heat of the kiln. Otherwise, the mold could slip out of the flask during the burnout. In lining the flask, asbestos should be moistened so that it will not decrease the amount of moisture in the mold material, causing it to crumble.

---

[44] Von Neumann, *op. cit.*, pp. 78-79.

Flasks improvised from tin cans

Casting flask lined with asbestos

INVESTING THE MODEL

The material used to make the mold for centrifugal casting is called investment. Similar in nature to plaster of Paris, this material mixes and sets in much the same manner. However, unlike plaster, it is especially suitable for casting because it possesses properties which enable it to withstand heat and other conditions to which it is subjected. Component parts of investment are plaster, which acts as a binder; silica, which lends high refractory properties; boric acid, which gives uniform thermal change during burnout; and graphite, which prevents oxidation. This composition results in an investment which sets in a firm, smooth contact with the wax model. Yet the mold material is porous enough to allow gases to move out ahead of the molten metal. It does not break down, crumble, or soften under high temperatures unless heated for long periods of time above 1350°F. With proper mixing and heating it possesses a crushing strength of 1500 pounds per square inch, strong enough to withstand casting shock.[45]

Investment is supplied in powder form by distributors of casting equipment, and is combined with water to form a pouring mixture of a creamy consistency. Water for mixing investment should be drawn from the faucet and allowed to stand for at least an hour before mixing. This will insure that the water will be at room temperature, or approximately 70°-80° F, which is considered the best temperature for mixing. Higher temperatures will accelerate the setting time, while lower temperatures will retard setting. Either extreme may affect the quality of the casting.

It is desirable to mix the investment in a rubber bowl designed for that purpose or improvised by cutting a child's rubber ball in half. The rubber mixing container facilitates the removal of any investment which hardens inside the bowl. Its flexibility causes dried investment to flake off.

In mixing, the water is first poured into the bowl, then the powdered investment is gradually sprinkled into the water and allowed to settle to the bottom. The exact water-powder ratio is 1 part water to 2.2 parts investment for cristobalite investment. However, exact measurement is not so important for our purposes as it would be in dental casting. With experience one is able to produce a successful investment mixture without such exact measurements. One method of obtaining a satisfactory mixture is to measure

---

[45] Von Neumann, *op. cit.*, p. 79.

Water with correct amount of investment added before mixing

the correct amount of water (about two-thirds enough to fill the flask), then gradually add sufficient investment powder to absorb all the standing water. All of the investment should be added before beginning the mixing process. If more investment powder is added after the chemical reaction has begun, the mold material will not set properly.

The investment may be mixed with a mechanical mixer or by hand using a spatula or the hand submerged in the bowl of investment. Care should be taken not to stir air into the mixture. The better the investment is mixed, the stronger the investment will be, and the smoother the surface of the finished casting will be.

When the water and investment have been combined into a creamy mixture, some method should be em-

Rubber bowl, spatula, and mechanical mixer for preparing investment for casting

ployed to remove air bubbles from the mixture. This may be accomplished by vibration. The most effective way to vibrate the investment is with a machine designed for that purpose. The vibrator consists essentially of a platform which is set in a vibrating motion by the use of electric current. When the rubber bowl containing the investment mixture is set on this platform, air entrapped in the mixture rises to the surface, and the bubbles may easily be broken up.

If a mechanical vibrator is not available, the same effect can be accomplished to some degree by a constant tapping with a rubber mallet on the bench top where the bowl of investment sits.

When removing air from the mixture by vibration, a mechanical mixer professionally designed for this

Removing air from the investment mixture by hand vibration

purpose may be used to remove further air from the mixture after vibration. The mechanical mixer consists of a rubber bowl with an airtight lid to which a handle is attached for operating a mixing apparatus inside the bowl. Because of the small size of the mixer, it may be necessary to fill the bowl twice. It is necessary to operate the mechanical mixer for only thirty seconds, thereby leaving ample time for the operation before the investment begins the chemical setting reaction.

Another method, and by far the best, of removing air from the mixture is that of using a vacuum pump. The investment is subjected to vacuum pressure two times: first as a mixture in the bowl and a second time after it is poured into the flask. The bowl of investment or the flask is placed under a bell jar, and the vacuum pump is employed to reduce air pressure inside the jar. When the pressure has been reduced sufficiently, air in the mixture exerts enough pressure to rise to the surface of the mixture. However, much of the air is eliminated by vapor pressure, for water at room temperature will boil when the air pressure is sufficiently reduced. The boiling, or vapor pressure, will completely eliminate all air. The bell jar rests on a base with a thin rubber top for an airtight fit, and this base is vibrated to loosen small air bubbles which cling to the wax impression.

If vacuuming is to be employed, it is necessary to build up the height of the flask by adding a retaining wall of rubber or paper because the investment rises in the flask as the air pressure inside the jar decreases.

If a vacuum pump is not available, the wax model should be painted with a coating of investment to avoid formation of air bubbles between the surface of the wax and the mold. Care should be taken that no air is trapped between the wax model and this thin coating of investment. Investment should be flowed onto the model with special attention to complex areas. The coating should be built up to a thickness of one-eighth inch or more. The investment should be about the consistency of heavy cream. In a thinner mixture there may be water separation, causing rough surfaces; a thicker mixture will not flow easily into areas of small detail.[46]

The investment-coated wax model should then be encased in the mold material or investment mixture by centering it inside a preselected

Wax model coated with investment

[46] Von Neumann, *op. cit.*, pp. 84-85.

flask. This may be accomplished in two ways. The wax model, mounted on the sprue former, may be set in an upright position and the flask centered over it to form a container for the investment. Investment is then poured around the model with care not to disturb it. The flask should be filled as full as possible, allowing the investment to rise slightly above the rim.

Investment-coated wax model inside flask

Flask filled with investment

The second manner of encasing the model in investment consists essentially of filling the flask and submerging the model into the prefilled flask. This is accomplished by placing the empty flask on a glass plate and sealing the point of juncture between the glass and the metal either with clay or softened wax. Investment is then poured into the flask, again filling it so that the investment rises slightly above the rim. The wax model is then inverted and lowered into the investment until the sprue former rests on the rim of the flask. Care should be taken that the cone-shaped portion of the sprue former rests directly in the center of the filled flask. Investment which overflows the rim of the flask as it is displaced by the wax model should be

Flask sealed to glass plate and filled with investment

Wax model mounted on sprue former inverted inside flask

left until setting is complete. One disadvantage of this method of investing the model is that air may become trapped between the investment and the sprue former leaving the sprue opening rough.

The investment should be allowed to stand for approximately one hour depending on the investment used. After initial setting, the sprue former may be gently removed from the flask by tapping or twisting, and the spilled investment scraped from the outside of the flask. The mold is now ready for the burnout. If it is not desired to do the burnout at this time, it may be done later. Twelve to twenty-four hours are not too long to wait, but if more than four hours elapse before the burnout, the mold should be immersed in water for a few minutes preceding the heating procedure to prevent drying and cracking of the investment during the burnout. The moisture also creates steam which aids in the elimination of wax from the mold.

Hardened mold ready for the casting process

BALANCING THE CASTING MACHINE

Before beginning the burnout process, the centrifugal casting machine must be balanced for the actual casting. The centrifugal casting machine is an apparatus which causes the arm holding the metal and the mold to revolve at a rate of approximately 300 revolutions per minute, forcing the metal into the mold by centrifugal force.

It is important that the machine be carefully mounted so that it is perfectly level and free from vibration when in use. Bolting it to a bench twenty to thirty inches from the floor makes it easy to attend during casting. A tilted machine loses much of its centrifugal force, and the main bearings could be seriously damaged. It is wise to oil the main shaft with light machine oil before each casting.

Since most machines operate on a horizontal axis, a barrier of sheet metal should be constructed to prevent accidents caused by excess hot metal which may be thrown from the machine. If desired, a slot may be left open at the front of the machine to allow easier access in melting the metal and releasing the spring. In this case, the operator should step to one side at the moment of releasing for his protection. Some craftsmen solve the problem of protection by mounting the machine in an ash bucket or garbage can bolting it through to a solid surface.

If a professional casting machine is not available, one may be constructed using an old top loading washing machine, a large pulley wheel, and a one-fourth horsepower motor, plus an iron elbow and arm.[47]

Centrifugal casting machine

[47] David P. Hatch, Correspondence to the author, March 5, 1962.

To balance the illustrated casting machine, the retaining nut in the center of the arm is loosened and weight is equally distributed on either end of the arm. The proper cradle and flask (with investment) are placed in position. The premeasured metal is placed in the clay crucible, which in turn rests in the crucible carrier. The crucible is pushed tight against the flask, care being taken to see that the sprue hole is in line with the hole in the crucible. Then the weights on the counterbalance end of the machine are manipulated to achieve a balance of weight between the two ends. When the arm is balanced, the retaining nut should be tightened.

Crucible, flask, and metal in position for casting

Counterbalance end of the centrifugal casting machine

BURNING OUT THE WAX

The burnout period has as its purpose the elimination of wax from the mold to form a negative of the model. A second function of the burnout is to mature the investment. In order to withstand casting shock, the investment must be strengthened by heating to a temperature of approximately 1200° F. The burnout also serves the purpose of attaining the proper mold temperature for the actual casting procedure. This period is very important because of the physical and chemical changes which occur in the investment as it goes through the heating stages.

In order to expel the wax from the investment, a furnace capable of reaching a temperature of at least 1300° F should be used. A front loading kiln facilitates handling of the flask. The ideal kiln for the melt-out process is a gas-fired, vented muffle oven. Small electric kilns may be used quite successfully also, but protection should be initiated for the heating elements because deposits caused by casting moisture and burning wax will damage them. The elements may be protected by the use of a metal or fire-clay muffle, as well as some method of ventilating gases. If necessary a kiln without a muffle or ventilating device may be used, utilizing the door for ventilation. However, such equipment affords greater opportunity for oxidation.[48] Good ventilation in the room where burnout is underway is doubly important because smoke resulting from the burning wax contains acrylic acid which is highly toxic.

An accurate pyrometer is desirable for successful burnout, and a rheostat control is helpful in maintaining

Flask in kiln for burnout process

[48] Von Neumann, *op. cit.*, pp. 80-82.

the correct heat level at any stage during the burnout. This device frees the craftsman from constant supervision of the kiln throughout the burnout process.

If desired, trivets of refractory clay or stainless steel may be used to support flasks above the kiln floor in the melt-out process. Additional equipment includes an asbestos glove and long handled flask tongs to be used in handling the hot flask.

For the burnout, the mold should be placed in a kiln with the sprue down so that wax may flow out when heated. The flask should be gradually raised from room temperature to 1300° F. In the interest of time, the kiln may be preheated to 800° F, if desired, but the mold may be distorted if placed in a kiln heated to a higher temperature. Under no circumstances should the

mold ever be heated to a temperature higher than 1350° F during the burnout. At 800° F the wax will burn from the mold, but a carbon residue will be left in the pores of the investment causing it to appear dirty. Continued heating is necessary to eliminate this residue from the pores, leaving them open, so that as metal comes in during the casting process, the air that is displaced can freely pass through the mold in every direction. The appearance of investment will serve as a reliable indicator of whether or not the carbon residue is completely eliminated. Dark areas on the surface of the investment indicate that carbon still remains and that the mold should be left in the kiln for a longer period of time or taken to a higher temperature.

-The length of time required for the burnout will depend on the amount of investment in the flask. Very small flasks may safely be raised to casting temperature or maturation temperature for investment (1300° F) in two hours. However, large flasks may require longer burnout periods if all traces of wax are to be eliminated without cracking of the investment from uneven expansion and stress.

The burnout may also be accomplished successfully with an open flame if a kiln is not available. The flask should be heated with a torch until all traces of wax and carbon have disappeared and the sprue holes are red hot.

The proper temperature for the flask at actual casting time is related to the melting temperature of the metal to be cast. The flask temperature is high enough to keep the metal in a fluid condition while it travels through the feed lines into the mold cavity. Yet, the mold is cool enough to allow the metal to solidify once it has reached the cavity. If a low casting temperature is required, the flask should be cooled to the desired temperature after it has been raised to 1300° F. Desired flask temperatures may be reached by bringing the kiln to the specified temperatures and "soaking" the flask at that temperature for at least half an hour to assure that it has attained the temperature indicated by the pyrometer. Flask temperatures desirable for casting various metals are as follows: Sterling silver can be cast into a flask with a temperature of from 700° to 1200° F. For optimum results, 900° is recommended. Gold is usually cast at a flask temperature of from 600° to

*Carbon deposit on investment
indicating improper burnout*

800° F. Tin, pewter and other low melting point metals can be cast into a cold flask without danger.[49]

While the mold is in the kiln for the burnout process, additional preparation for casting may be made. The mold should be left in the kiln until just before setting the casting machine in motion.

[49] Wright, *op. cit.*, p. 66.

FINAL PREPARATION AND CASTING

Cleaning the metal

In preparation for casting, it is desirable that the premeasured metal be thoroughly cleaned to free it of grease and oxides. This may be ac-complished by annealing the metal and dropping it in a pickling solution. The pickling solution should be rinsed from the metal, and it should be painted with a coating of flux to prevent oxidation and aid in the flow of the metal while it is in a molten state.

Lining the crucible

The refractory crucible which will hold the molten metal may be lined with asbestos to aid in the melting of the metal and to prevent the metal from picking up foreign particles. Asbestos is cut to fit the floor of the crucible, moistened, and molded into place. The asbestos may be molded to build up the back wall slightly at the shallow end of the crucible, especially if a large quantity of metal is to be used.

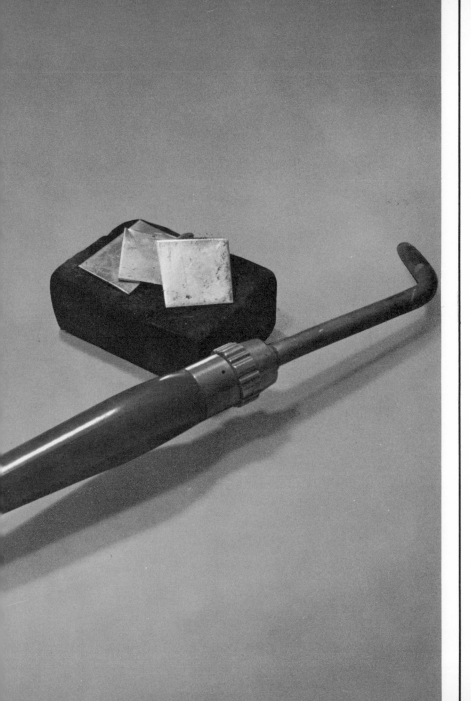

Cleaning the metal before casting

Coating the metal with flux

Varying sizes of crucibles

Separate crucibles should be used for different metals. Do not allow crucibles to become caked with flux. Should this happen, the flux may be dissolved in boiling water or simply scraped away. The lined crucible should be placed in the crucible carrier and filled with the metal.

Winding the machine

The casting machine must be wound in preparation for casting. The arm assembly should be given two and one-half to four complete turns. The arm is then locked in place with the stop rod which is provided for that purpose. To facilitate effective working during the casting procedure, the machine should be stopped so that the crucible faces the operator across from the retaining nut.

Crucible lined with asbestos in preparation for casting

Melting the metal in preparation for casting

Melting the metal

After the flask reaches the desired temperature for casting, the metal is melted in the crucible. A gas torch is used to melt the metal, except in those cases where the casting machine is equipped with its own furnace. The torch may be oxy-acetylene, oxygen-gas, or air-gas.

The metal must not be overheated. It should be melted only a little above its flow point. The metal should appear shiny on the surface and should move easily if the arm of the machine is shaken gently. However, it should never spin or boil. Overheating of the metal increases shrinkage during cooling, and thus makes more likely the possibility of porosity in the casting. Impurities should be removed from the surface of the molten metal with a slate pencil or a steel rod.

Placing the flask in position and releasing the machine

When the metal is properly melted, the flask should be removed from the kiln with tongs and placed in position on the machine, carefully sliding the crucible against the flask so that the hole in the crucible is in alignment with the sprue through which molten metal will enter the mold cavity. With the flask in position, heat should once again be concentrated on the metal to ascertain that it has reached the proper liquid state. At that time the arm should be moved slightly in a clockwise direction to release the stop rod, which will drop into the base of the machine. Simultaneously the torch should be removed and the arm released, setting the machine in motion. The machine will continue to spin for two to five minutes. It should be allowed to spin until it stops naturally.

Placing the heated flask in position for casting

Centrifugal casting machine in motion

Cooling and cleaning the casting

After the machine has stopped, tongs should be used to remove the flask from the machine. It may be desirable to set the flask aside to cool for a short period, depending on the metal used. With silver, however, the casting may be removed immediately. The higher the melting point of the metal used, the longer the cooling period to any given temperature. The flask may then be immersed in a bucket or pan containing enough water to completely cover the flask. With the sudden change in temperature, most investment will break up and leave the casting free. The cast piece may then be cleaned with a stiff brush, and the investment removed from the flask. The casting should be annealed to a dull red glow, then pickled in an acid solution appropriate to the metal.

Flask submerged in water for cooling

Sterling silver may be cleaned in a solution of sulfuric acid (1 part) and water (10 parts). Gold should be pickled in hydrochloric acid (1 part) and water (10 parts). If the casting is left for several hours, a solution of 50% sodium citrate and 50% water will clean away all investment and remove oxidation. After the acid solution has been washed from the piece, it is ready for refining and polishing.

Sprues and excess metal may be cut from the casting with a jeweler's saw, or shears before polishing.

Refining of the pieces is accomplished with files or an electric hand drill, or flexible shaft, with accompanying accessories. Final polishing of the cast piece is accomplished as in other jewelry processes, by the use of a polishing compound and either a soft cloth or an electric polishing wheel.

Casting as removed from flask

Finished cast piece

REFERENCE MATERIALS

BIBLIOGRAPHY

Books:

Beitler, Ethel J., and Lockhart, Bill C., *Design for You.* New York, John Wiley & Sons, Inc., 1961.

Bovin, Murray. *Jewelry Making for Schools, Tradesmen, Craftsmen.* Forest Hills, Long Island, Murray Bovin, 1960.

Dewey, John. *Art as Experience.* Reprinted by permission of G. P. Putnam's Sons. New York, Milton, Balch & Company, 1934.

Faulkner, Ray, Ziegfield, Edwin, and Hill, Gerald, *Art Today.* New York, Henry Holt & Company, Inc., 1958.

Handbook of Chemistry and Physics, Charles D. Hodgman, ed. Cleveland, Chemical Rubber Publishing Company, 1956.

Pack, Greta, *Jewelry and Enameling.* Princeton, D. Van Nostrand Company, Inc., 1953.

Teague, Walter Dorwin, *Design This Day*. London, The Studio Publications, 1946.

Von Neumann, Robert. *The Design and Creation of Jewelry*. Copyright, 1961, by the author. Reprinted with permission of the publisher. Philadelphia, Chilton Books, 1961.

Winebrenner, D. Kenneth, *Jewelry Making as an Art Expression*. Scranton, International Textbook Company, 1955.

Booklets:

Directions for Using Kerr Centrifico Casting Machine. Detroit, Kerr Manufacturing Company.

Fine Jewelry, Casting Equipment and Supplies. New York, Alexander Saunders and Company.

Lost Wax, the New Modern Craft. Detroit, Kerr Manufacturing Company.

Satin Cast Investment. Detroit, Kerr Manufacturing Company.

Unpublished Master's Theses:

Krentzin, Earl. *Centrifugal Casting of Hollow Objects*. Bloomfield Hills: Cranbrook Academy of Art Library, 1954.

Lawson, Gordon C. *Form in Silver*. Bloomfield Hills: Cranbrook Academy of Art Library, 1950.

Saunderson, Wiley D., Jr. *Metal Expression Through Centrifugal Casting*. Bloomfield Hills: Cranbrook Academy of Art Library, 1949.

Thomas, Richard C. *Alloys.* Bloomfield Hills: Cranbrook Academy of Art Library, 1948.

Wright, Donald B. *Centrifugal Investment Casting for the Artist-Craftsman.* Bloomfield Hills: Cranbrook Academy of Art Library, 1958.

Periodicals:

Brown, Conrad, "J. Arnold Frew." *Craft Horizons,* XVIII (January/February, 1958), pp. 34-36.

Brown, Conrad, "Henry Shawah's Jewelry is a Compliment to Beauty." *Craft Horizons,* XIX (September/October, 1959), pp. 33-34.

Krevitsky, Nik, "Winston's Cast Forms." *Craft Horizons,* XXII (January/February, 1962), pp. 10-12.

Lair, Felt, "Jewelry by Christian Schmidt." *Craft Horizons,* XX (May/June, 1960), pp. 25-27.

Rabchuk, Alexander, "Uniform Results from Investment Casting." *The American Jewelry Manufacturer,* June, 1960 (reprint).

"Radakovich," *Craft Horizons,* XVIII (September/October, 1958), pp. 25-31.

Rhodes, Daniel, "Form in Silver by Ronald Pearson." *Craft Horizons,* XX (November/December, 1960), pp. 19-21.

Slivka, Rose, "Irena Brynner." *Craft Horizons, XIX* (March/April, 1959), pp. 33-35.

SUPPLY SOURCES

Alexander Saunders and
   Company, Inc.
95 Bedford Street
New York 14, New York

Casting Supply House
62 West 47th Street
New York 36, New York

The Cleveland Dental
   Manufacturing Company
3307 Scranton Road
Cleveland 1, Ohio

The I. Shor Company, Inc.
64 West 48th Street
New York 36, New York

Jelrus Technical Products
   Corporation
2020 Jericho Turnpike
New Hyde Park, New York

Kerr Manufacturing Company
6081-6095 Twelfth Street
Detroit 8, Michigan

GLOSSARY OF TERMS

Bell jar and vacuum pump—a mechanical device used to remove air from investment by vacuum pressure

Burnout—the period, prior to casting, in which the investment-filled flask is heated with a two-fold purpose: 1) formation of a negative mold of the wax model and 2) maturation of the investment

Centrifugal casting machine—a mechanically-driven apparatus which causes an arm, holding metal and a mold, to revolve at a rate of 300 rpm, centrifugally forcing the metal into the mold

Centrifuge—centrifugal casting machine

Cire-perdue—lost-wax method of casting

Crucible—highly refractory container in which metal is melted for casting

Debubblizer—a solution which acts as a wetting agent, relieving the surface tension of a wax model and allowing more accurate adhesion of the investment to the model

Fabrication—jewelry process in which the piece is built up of stock metal, such as sheet, wire, tube, etc.

Flask—metal cylinder holding investment, in which the wax model is encased to form a mold

Flux—a substance used in jewelry processes to prevent the oxidation of metal in the presence of heat and to aid in the flow of solder; used in casting to aid the flow of molten metal

Fusing—joining metal by heating it to a molten state so that it flows together

Investment—material, similar to plaster of Paris, used to make the mold for centrifugal casting; possesses qualities which make it especially suitable for casting

Kiln—small oven used (in casting process) for burnout

Lost wax—casting process in which a previously prepared wax model is burned away to form a mold into which metal is later forced

Mohs scale—scale established by Moh, a mineralogist, to indicate the hardness of stones and minerals

Pickle—solution used by jewelers to clean metals

Pyrometer—device which indicates the degree of heat in a kiln

Retaining nut—nut in center of arm on casting machine, which holds the arm in place and is loosened to facilitate the balancing of the machine

Rheostat control—device designed to maintain a desired degree of heat in a kiln

Ring mandrel—a tapered steel bar around which rings are formed

Shank—band portion of a ring

Sprue former—circular metal plate, with cone shape in center, used to form in investment the opening to channels through which molten metal will flow during the casting process

Sprues—linear wax appendages attached to the wax model; when invested and burned out, sprues form in the mold hollow channels through which, during the casting process, molten metal flows to the negative space originally occupied by the wax model

Wax model—a pattern, in exact detail, of a piece of jewelry to be cast; from this model is formed a negative mold into which molten metal is forced

INDEX